MATT CHANDLER

THE MINGLING of SOULS

Study Guide

A Study of Attraction, Love, Marriage & Redemption from Song of Solomon.

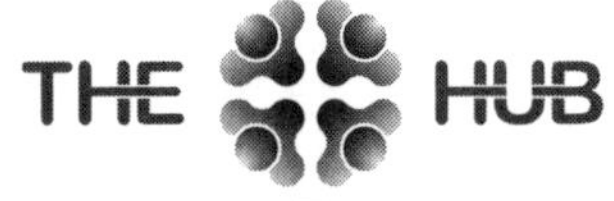

Published 2011
by

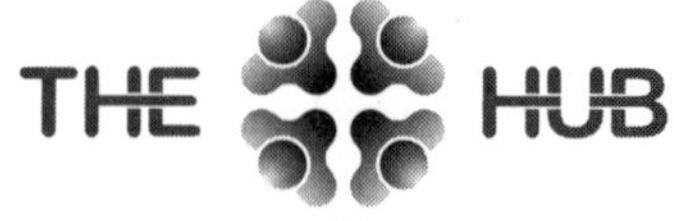

www.gotothehub.com

3405 Milton Avenue, Suite 207
Dallas, TX 75205

Printed in the United States

BIBLE STUDIES

BUY.RENT.DOWNLOAD

ECCLESIASTES

A Life Well Lived (A Study of Ecclesiastes)
Bible Study Series by Tommy Nelson
- 4 DVD Curriculum
- Companion Study Guide
- A Life Well Lived paperback book

PHILIPPIANS

NEW! Philippians, To Live is Christ & to Die is Gain
Bible Study Series by Matt Chandler
- 4 DVD Curriculum
- Companion Study Guide
- Packages and bulk discounts available

ROMANS

NEW! Romans, The Letter that Changed the World, Vol. I and II
Bible Study Series by Tommy Nelson
- DVD Curriculum
- Companion Study Guide
- Packages and bulk discounts available

RUTH

NEW! Ruth; Your God, My God. A True Story of Love & Redemption
Bible Study Series by Tommy Nelson
- 4 DVD Curriculum
- Companion Study Guide
- Packages and bulk discounts available

SONG OF SOLOMON

NEW and Improved! 1995 Song of Solomon Classic
DVD Curriculum by Tommy Nelson
- Enhanced video, audio and color graphics
- Updated and enlarged companion Study Guide
- Formatted for Widescreen

NEW! Enhanced SOS for Students
DVD Curriculum by Tommy Nelson
- Re-Mastered Video & Audio
- All new graphics and menus
- Never before seen Q & A's
- All in one Study Guide for both Students & Leaders

VINTAGE JESUS

NEW! Vintage Jesus, Timeless Answers to Timely Questions
Bible Study Series by Mark Driscoll
- 4 DVD Curriculum
- Companion Study Guide
- Packages and bulk discounts available

ACKNOWLEDGEMENTS

The Hub wishes to thank the following friends, without whose help, this series and study guide would not have been possible:

Jim Gribnitz, Crosswise Media (Study Guide Consultant) • **Matt Coleman**, Unblind Productions, Producer • **Drew Rodgers**, Livingstone Designs • **Shatrine Krake**, Krake Designs • **Sandy Orellana** • **Jason Countryman**, PocketPak Albums • **Woodlands Church, Pastor Kerry Shook** and entire Media Staff

ABOUT THE HUB

Thanks for taking a moment to learn more about us. Our organization began in 1995 working with one speaker, Tommy Nelson and one amazing message, The Song of Solomon. It was and is our privilege to help champion God's written Word on Love, Dating, Marriage and Sex based directly on Song of Solomon. It is a book that has been censored for centuries and it has been a total blessing and thrill to see it change my life, and millions of others.

As of August 2009 we have rebranded our organization to reflect the root of our passion and the future of our organization:

To Develop, Find and Share life changing Bible Centric tools that move people forward. We have renamed our organization to The Hub. It is our passion and commitment to be a Hub for unique, challenging and grace filled resources. I hope you will agree after you participate and interact with one of our resources. God Bless you and know that if you will listen, God's Truth will move you forward in life, no matter where you have been or are currently.

Doug Hudson, President - The Hub

TABLE OF CONTENTS

ABOUT THE AUTHOR

MATT CHANDLER serves as Lead Pastor of The Village Church in Highland Village, TX. He describes his tenure at The Village as a re-planting effort where he was involved in changing the theological and philosophical culture of the congregation.

The church has witnessed a tremendous response growing from 160 people to over 8,000 including satellite campuses in Dallas and Denton. He is one of the most downloaded teachers on iTunes and consistently remains in the Top 5 of all national Religion and Spirituality Podcasts.

Matt's passion is to speak to people in America and abroad about the glory of God and beauty of Jesus.

His greatest joy outside of Jesus is being married to Lauren and being a dad to their three children, Audrey, Reid and Norah.

A NOTE

I like sports quite a bit, though I quickly realized that I was much better at reading than I was at athletics, so I became a pastor.

I'm constantly amazed at the profound effect that sports has on us as a culture, especially as men. When our teams win, we are on cloud nine, and when they lose, we crumble.

(I'm still trying to figure out why we let a bunch of boys throwing a ball into a hoop after bouncing it well on the floor have a huge impact on us, but I digress…)

Literally millions of dollars and millions of people's happiness are determined by the oddest bounce, one bad call by a ref, or someone stumbling for a tenth of a second. The highs and lows of following a sports team are remarkable. So much joy and so much pain for so many people rises and falls on such random minutiae.

Seems the same way with love…

The way we have done 'love' for centuries now is that it is a precarious thing, and emotions can rise and fall with a simple glance, touch, kiss, or word. Little things cause violent emotional responses, and romance, dating, sex and marriage can be our source of the highest highs or the lowest lows – and those can happen within moments of each other.

These are deep, dangerous waters we are in, and luckily the One who has created all this mystery, also desires to help us navigate.

Buckle up.

1

THE MINGLING *of* SOULS

Genesis 1-2; Song of Solomon 1:1-12

INTRO

Three quick things that, I promise, are related:

1) I always giggle at fitness commercials when they promise something for nothing. Fitness companies are clearly competing to see who can convince the buyer that they give them the absolute highest reward for the absolute lowest cost. They are having a 'crazy' contest to see who can make the most outlandish promises, like "lose 400 pounds in just three minutes a day for 2 days, and never change your eating habits."

2) I fear for my children as they grow up watching athletes that seem to have it all despite never having gone to college and not being able to use any semblance of proper grammar in an interview. I fear my kids think they will secretly or openly expect to get what they have and only be asked to pay a very small price. These superstars and movie stars appear to have gotten 'something' with no discernible talent or effort.

3) So many newly married couples set their expectations for their first home at what their parents currently have. They overlook the fact that their parents have spent 30 years accumulating wealth by saving and spending wisely in order to afford what they have now. Young couples want what their parents have but are annoyed when asked to put in the effort.

All three of these have one thing in common: we all want a huge reward yet pay no price to get it.

Relationships with the opposite sex are the same way. We want something but are unwilling to pay a price for it. We want to hurry ahead to the 'good' stuff, instead of putting in the sweat at the beginning, 'not-so-fun' parts.

We often just want the chemistry to be there, for everything to just naturally happen, and for there to be no real work on our part except that which we want to do anyway.

Flying in the face of this: The relationships that God intends for us to have require doing some things we would rather not do. We want to start on step 4, skipping over 1-3. But we can't.

The basics that we are about to look at are absolutely vital.

Don't breeze through them quickly. Soak in them for a while.

THE WORD

GENESIS 1:1-28

GENESIS 1

1 In the beginning, God created the heavens and the earth. 2 The earth was without form
and void, and darkness was over the face of the deep. And the Spirit of God was hover-
ing over the face of the waters. 3 And God said, "Let there be light," and there was light.
4 And God saw that the light was good. And God separated the light from the darkness.
5 God called the light Day, and the darkness he called Night. And there was evening and
there was morning, the first day. 6 And God said, "Let there be an expanse in the midst of
the waters, and let it separate the waters from the waters." 7 And God made the expanse
and separated the waters that were under the expanse from the waters that were above
the expanse. And it was so. 8 And God called the expanse Heaven. And there was evening and there was morning, the second day. 9 And God said, "Let the waters under the
heavens be gathered together into one place, and let the dry land appear." And it was
so. 10 God called the dry land Earth, and the waters that were gathered together he called
Seas. And God saw that it was good. 11 And God said, "Let the earth sprout vegetation,
plants yielding seed, and fruit trees bearing fruit in which is their seed, each according to
its kind, on the earth." And it was so. 12 The earth brought forth vegetation, plants yielding seed according to their own kinds, and trees bearing fruit in which is their seed, each
according to its kind. And God saw that it was good. 13 And there was evening and there
was morning, the third day. 14 And God said, "Let there be lights in the expanse of the
heavens to separate the day from the night. And let them be for signs and for seasons,
and for days and years, 15 and let them be lights in the expanse of the heavens to give light
upon the earth." And it was so. 16 And God made the two great lights—the greater light
to rule the day and the lesser light to rule the night—and the stars. 17 And God set them in
the expanse of the heavens to give light on the earth, 18 to rule over the day and over the
night, and to separate the light from the darkness. And God saw that it was good. 19 And
there was evening and there was morning, the fourth day. 20 And God said, "Let the waters
swarm with swarms of living creatures, and let birds fly above the earth across the expanse
of the heavens." 21 So God created the great sea creatures and every living creature that
moves, with which the waters swarm, according to their kinds, and every winged bird according to its kind. And God saw that it was good. 22 And God blessed them, saying, "Be
fruitful and multiply and fill the waters in the seas, and let birds multiply on the earth."
23 And there was evening and there was morning, the fifth day. 24 And God said, "Let the
earth bring forth living creatures according to their kinds—livestock and creeping things
and beasts of the earth according to their kinds." And it was so. 25 And God made the
beasts of the earth according to their kinds and the livestock according to their kinds,
and everything that creeps on the ground according to its kind. And God saw that it was
good. 26 Then God said, "Let us make man[h] in our image, after our likeness. And let them
have dominion over the fish of the sea and over the birds of the heavens and over the
livestock and over all the earth and over every creeping thing that creeps on the earth."
27 So God created man in his own image, in the image of God he created him; male and
female he created them. 28 And God blessed them. And God said to them, "Be fruitful and
multiply and fill the earth and subdue it and have dominion over the fish of the sea and

THE WORD

GENESIS 1:29-2:24

over the birds of the heavens and over every living thing that moves on the earth." [29]And God said, "Behold, I have given you every plant yielding seed that is on the face of all the earth, and every tree with seed in its fruit. You shall have them for food. [30]And to every beast of the earth and to every bird of the heavens and to everything that creeps on the earth, everything that has the breath of life, I have given every green plant for food." And it was so. [31]And God saw everything that he had made, and behold, it was very good. And there was evening and there was morning, the sixth day.

GENESIS 2

[1]Thus the heavens and the earth were finished, and all the host of them. [2]And on the seventh day God finished his work that he had done, and he rested on the seventh day from all his work that he had done. [3]So God blessed the seventh day and made it holy, because on it God rested from all his work that he had done in creation. [4]These are the generations of the heavens and the earth when they were created, in the day that the LORD God made the earth and the heavens. [5]When no bush of the field was yet in the land and no small plant of the field had yet sprung up—for the LORD God had not caused it to rain on the land, and there was no man to work the ground, [6]and a mist was going up from the land and was watering the whole face of the ground— [7]then the LORD God formed the man of dust from the ground and breathed into his nostrils the breath of life, and the man became a living creature. [8]And the LORD God planted a garden in Eden, in the east, and there he put the man whom he had formed. [9]And out of the ground the LORD God made to spring up every tree that is pleasant to the sight and good for food. The tree of life was in the midst of the garden, and the tree of the knowledge of good and evil. [10]A river flowed out of Eden to water the garden, and there it divided and became four rivers. [11]The name of the first is the Pishon. It is the one that flowed around the whole land of Havilah, where there is gold. [12]And the gold of that land is good; bdellium and onyx stone are there. [13]The name of the second river is the Gihon. It is the one that flowed around the whole land of Cush. [14]And the name of the third river is the Tigris, which flows east of Assyria. And the fourth river is the Euphrates. [15]The LORD God took the man and put him in the garden of Eden to work it and keep it. [16]And the LORD God commanded the man, saying, "You may surely eat of every tree of the garden, [17]but of the tree of the knowledge of good and evil you shall not eat, for in the day that you eat of it you shall surely die."[18]Then the LORD God said, "It is not good that the man should be alone; I will make him a helper fit for him." [19]Now out of the ground the LORD God had formed every beast of the field and every bird of the heavens and brought them to the man to see what he would call them. And whatever the man called every living creature, that was its name. [20]The man gave names to all livestock and to the birds of the heavens and to every beast of the field. But for Adam there was not found a helper fit for him. [21]So the LORD God caused a deep sleep to fall upon the man, and while he slept took one of his ribs and closed up its place with flesh. [22]And the rib that the LORD God had taken from the man he made into a woman and brought her to the man. [23]Then the man said, "This at last is bone of my bones and flesh of my flesh; she shall be called Woman, because she was taken out of Man." [24]Therefore a man shall leave his father and his mother and hold

THE WORD

GENESIS 2:25; SONG OF SOLOMON 1:1-12

fast to his wife, and they shall become one flesh. 25 And the man and his wife were both
naked and were not ashamed.

SONG OF SOLOMON 1:1-12

1 The Song of Songs, which is Solomon's. 2 Let him kiss me with the kisses of his mouth! For
your love is better than wine; 3 your anointing oils are fragrant; your name is oil poured out;
therefore virgins love you. 4 Draw me after you; let us run. The king has brought me into his
chambers. We will exult and rejoice in you; we will extol your love more than wine; rightly
do they love you. 5 I am very dark, but lovely, O daughters of Jerusalem, like the tents of
Kedar, like the curtains of Solomon. 6 Do not gaze at me because I am dark, because the
sun has looked upon me. My mother's sons were angry with me; they made me keeper
of the vineyards, but my own vineyard I have not kept! 7 Tell me, you whom my soul loves,
where you pasture your flock, where you make it lie down at noon; for why should I be
like one who veils herself beside the flocks of your companions? 8 If you do not know, O
most beautiful among women, follow in the tracks of the flock, and pasture your young
goats beside the shepherds' tents. 9 I compare you, my love, to a mare among Pharaoh's
chariots. 10 Your cheeks are lovely with ornaments, your neck with strings of jewels. 11 We will
make for you ornaments of gold, studded with silver. 12 While the king was on his couch,
my nard gave forth its fragrance.

DISCUSSION *Questions*

1. We mention several things that are intended by God for our pleasure and we have corrupted them and they have become sinful and/or harmful (wine becomes alcoholism, food becomes gluttony, sex becomes something that causes heartache, etc.). What other things are meant as perhaps good gifts from God, but have been corrupted by the world and instead cause pain?

"There has been more sorrow and pain in the lives of men and women that have pursued physical attraction alone."

2. What are some of the other major differences you see between little boys and little girls? Are they significant?

"Ladies, when a man has a history of devastation, and you are going to be his savior, that is absurd."

3. *Ladies first:* describe some characteristics of a man with a good 'name', or reputation. What is he like? Conversely, what are some key things you can see in men that would indicate they have poor character? *Men*, now you do the same for the ladies.

4. *Ladies (especially):* seeing a man with a poor track record, yet thinking you can be the one to 'fix' him is obviously faulty logic. Why do so many women continue to think that they can be the exception? What is the deception within this predicament that allows them to slip into this over and over?

"Almost every issue we deal with in counseling, they both saw it when they were dating, but they both thought they could fix it afterwards."

5. Discuss these two seemingly contradictory statements from the culture: There seems to be a stigma in our culture against those that say they desire to be married. Also, our culture is very big on 'do whatever makes you happy'.

"Any preacher or pastor who teaches the Bible and tells you that it is sinful to want to be married is absurd."

6. *Men:* note the progression the author gives us for how she 'selects' a man. She does have a physical attraction, then her friends give hearty approval to him, she observes his character over time, and then – oops – 'accidentally' crosses paths with him. Is the progression the same for a man with a woman? Is there anything missing or are one of these emphasized more than another?

7. You have no business dating if you haven't answered a few key questions: a) 'what do you want and what are you looking for?' and b) 'what you would be willing to wait on?' Pretend you are giving counsel to a young high school or college couple. How would you guide them to answer these questions?

"If you haven't said 'I'm willing to wait on this type of man', 'this is the kind of woman that I want to date', then I think you are really foolish for dating. You're playing with some things that, in the end, could blow you to kingdom come."

8. Simply discuss the concept of 'dode' meaning 'the mingling of souls'. What are the implications of this? How should the Christian perception of marriage shift as we look at marriage in this way?

"It's a weird thing to gamble the heart."

MEMORY VERSE

SONG OF SOLOMON 1:3
"Your anointing oils are fragrant; your name is oil poured out; therefore virgins love you."

DIVING *deeper*

HOMEWORK FOR MARRIED COUPLES: Often when it comes to Scriptures about marriage, we jump to 1 Corinthians 13, Ephesians 5, or 1 Peter 3. Men, tonight, read to your wife the creation account found in Genesis 1-2, expecting nothing in return. Just read the Scriptures over her and let her enjoy her husband taking this step of ownership in the faith of the family.

HOMEWORK FOR DATING, ENGAGED & SINGLES: Meditate on the Memory Verse about the greatness of the 'name' of the man…his reputation and character. What would others say about your character? Do enough people actually know you to that level? What steps could you take to make a 'name' for yourself?

PRAYER *Requests*

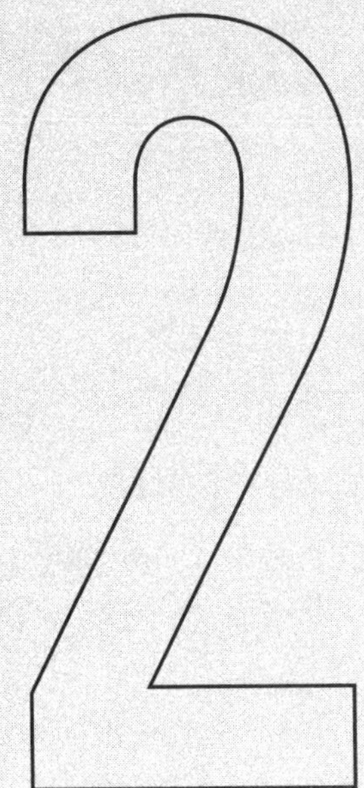

DATING *done* WELL

Song of Solomon 1:13-3:5

INTRO

I hear all the time that, 'everyone is different, and we are all individuals."

True.

However, having been a pastor now for several years, I can safely tell you that every single person in the world has one thing in common:

Everyone has issues.

Some have issues the size of Texas, some more Rhode Island-ish. Some have the same issue for their whole life, and some people change what their 'issues' are periodically. Some deal with them, and some bury them. Some name them and some act as though they do not exist. How we deal with them varies, but we all have them as individuals.

When we get together as a couple, the ignorant thing to do is to assume that your issues will somehow go away once you meet that special someone. Or believe that your issues will never come to light and never need to be dealt with.

We can ignore the issues, though that just means that we are settling for a terrible love life (among other things). We are physically able to suppress these things for a season if necessary, but they eventually rear their head given time.

But why wouldn't we look harder at our junk? Why wouldn't we deal with our issues upfront and honestly? Addressing our 'issues', childhood pain, short tempers, addictions, and more, is a vital step to having a dating life like God wants us to have.

We settle for mediocrity, and living in the fear that our dark will come to light.

Wise people know their issues, and bring them to light so that they can have – not just a dating experience, but a thriving one.

That is a key component to dating done right.

THE WORD

SONG OF SOLOMON 1:13-3:5

[13]My beloved is to me a sachet of myrrh that lies between my breasts. [14]My beloved is to me a cluster of henna blossoms in the vineyards of Engedi. [15]Behold, you are beautiful, my love; behold, you are beautiful; your eyes are doves. [16]Behold, you are beautiful, my beloved, truly delightful. Our couch is green; [17]the beams of our house are cedar; our rafters are pine.

SONG OF SOLOMON 2

[1]I am a rose of Sharon, a lily of the valleys. [2]As a lily among brambles, so is my love among the young women. [3]As an apple tree among the trees of the forest, so is my beloved among the young men. With great delight I sat in his shadow, and his fruit was sweet to my taste. [4]He brought me to the banqueting house, and his banner over me was love. [5]Sustain me with raisins; refresh me with apples, for I am sick with love. [6]His left hand is under my head, and his right hand embraces me! [7]I adjure you, O daughters of Jerusalem, by the gazelles or the does of the field, that you not stir up or awaken love until it pleases. [8]The voice of my beloved! Behold, he comes, leaping over the mountains, bounding over the hills. [9]My beloved is like a gazelle or a young stag. Behold, there he stands behind our wall, gazing through the windows, looking through the lattice. [10]My beloved speaks and says to me: "Arise, my love, my beautiful one, and come away, [11]for behold, the winter is past; the rain is over and gone. [12]The flowers appear on the earth, the time of singing[d] has come, and the voice of the turtledove is heard in our land. [13]The fig tree ripens its figs, and the vines are in blossom; they give forth fragrance. Arise, my love, my beautiful one, and come away. [14]O my dove, in the clefts of the rock, in the crannies of the cliff, let me see your face, let me hear your voice, for your voice is sweet, and your face is lovely. [15]Catch the foxes for us, the little foxes that spoil the vineyards, for our vineyards are in blossom." [16]My beloved is mine, and I am his; he grazes among the lilies. [17]Until the day breathes and the shadows flee, turn, my beloved, be like a gazelle or a young stag on cleft mountains.

SONG OF SOLOMON 3

[1]On my bed by night I sought him whom my soul loves; I sought him, but found him not. [2]I will rise now and go about the city, in the streets and in the squares; I will seek him whom my soul loves. I sought him, but found him not. [3]The watchmen found me as they went about in the city. "Have you seen him whom my soul loves?" [4]Scarcely had I passed them when I found him whom my soul loves. I held him, and would not let him go until I had brought him into my mother's house, and into the chamber of her who conceived me. [5]I adjure you, O daughters of Jerusalem, by the gazelles or the does of the field, that you not stir up or awaken love until it pleases.

DISCUSSION *Questions*

1.When does it move from 'casual' dating to 'exclusive' dating? How should that process be handled by the couple? Should they discuss it in detail? Who should initiate?

"You can't say that there is something beautiful about your soul, about your personhood, after one date."

2. *Song of Solomom 2:14* describes the fact that something came up in the past that caused one of them to 'hide' from the other. What are some things that a spouse or dating partner can do that would cause you and those of your gender to shrink away and 'hide'?

"I can't tell you how many 22 year old dudes come into my office asking that God take it (his sexual desire for women) away from him. Really?! You want him to take that away from you? You would rather choose to be indifferent?"

3. Issues need to be dealt with. What are healthy ways to deal with them for your gender? For the other gender? What are unhealthy, unhelpful, and hurtful ways of dealing with issues that your gender usually does to the other? What about the other gender to yours?

4. "Little foxes" are issues that need to be addressed. They eat away at our ability to communicate, walk in intimacy, and our ability to trust God. What else can 'little foxes' do to your relationships?

"If you still lack the ability to judge character, I don't know that you should move from casually dating to exclusively dating."

5. *Ladies:* can you give your perspective on the importance of trusting a man you are dating or married to. Where does it rank on your 'list'? What is the effect it has on you if you can trust him deeply? What if you can't? In what areas is this trust most vital?

"You should tap the brakes if, in your casual dating, you have run out of things to say."

6. What are the effects we see in culture of having made sex a purely physical encounter?

"I'm always worried about people who don't think there are issues at the engaged level."

"When you remove the relational element of sex, what you've done is absolutely destroyed any hope you have of sex being any semblance of genuine, legit intimacy."

7. *Discuss:* There is a perception that God is a "Cosmic Killjoy" (that we would clearly disagree with), however, He does give us parameters and guidelines, not permitting us to do things that He does not want. So…isn't He kind of a killjoy? How would you answer that to someone outside of the church?

"When you are making love to a soul and not a physical body there is this unbelievably powerful, fulfilling beautiful thing that occurs. When you are just having sex with a body, there is always an emptiness that follows."

MEMORYVERSE

SONG OF SOLOMON 2:15

"Catch the foxes for us, the little foxes that spoil the vineyards, for our vineyards are in blossom."

DIVING*deeper*

This week take note in the supermarket, television ads, internet ads, etc. of the messages that are sent about what sex is. How does that impact you? It impacts the society you live in, so it must shape you in some way!

PRAYER *Requests*

SEX IS ROMANTIC. Gentle. SENSUOUS. GODLY.

Song of Solomon 3:6-4:16

INTRO

My son is a fan of puzzles, but he didn't 'get' them right at first...

One day he came into the kitchen and found me, telling me that he was going to do a puzzle all by himself. He wanted to show me the result so I could tell him how proud I was of him.

I went in 30 minutes later when he had not come out, wondering what was going on, because it was one of those little kid puzzles with a total of about 4 pieces. This should not have taken so long. I went in to investigate.

Poor kid. I walked in and he was crying.

After some time of just holding him and letting him know that daddy was here, I asked him what the problem was. He said he could not do the puzzle and wanted to do it on his own, for me....

I had never seen the puzzle before, so I grabbed the box top and turned it over to look at the picture. His eyes lit up when he saw the picture on the box, and he did the puzzle in about 10 seconds.

He couldn't figure out the puzzle until I could show him the picture of what it should look like when he was done. How could he know how to do it right without a picture of what it should be?

God gives us a marvelous text that enables us to see what real, genuine biblical sex is, too. This chapter is the box top that lets us see some characteristics of sex so we can model our attitudes towards sex and each other after this couple.

THE WORD

SONG OF SOLOMON 3:6-4:16

6What is that coming up from the wilderness like columns of smoke, perfumed with myrrh
and frankincense, with all the fragrant powders of a merchant? 7Behold, it is the litter of
Solomon!Around it are sixty mighty men, some of the mighty men of Israel, 8all of them
wearing swords and expert in war, each with his sword at his thigh, against terror by night.
9King Solomon made himself a carriage from the wood of Lebanon. 10He made its posts
of silver, its back of gold, its seat of purple; its interior was inlaid with love by the daughters of Jerusalem. 11Go out, O daughters of Zion, and look upon King Solomon, with the
crown with which his mother crowned him on the day of his wedding, on the day of the
gladness of his heart.

SONG OF SOLOMON 4

1Behold, you are beautiful, my love, behold, you are beautiful! Your eyes are doves behind your veil. Your hair is like a flock of goats leaping down the slopes of Gilead. 2Your
teeth are like a flock of shorn ewes that have come up from the washing, all of which bear
twins, and not one among them has lost its young. 3Your lips are like a scarlet thread,
and your mouth is lovely. Your cheeks are like halves of a pomegranate behind your veil.
4Your neck is like the tower of David, built in rows of stone; on it hang a thousand shields,
all of them shields of warriors. 5Your two breasts are like two fawns, twins of a gazelle,
that graze among the lilies. 6Until the day breathes and the shadows flee, I will go away
to the mountain of myrrh and the hill of frankincense. 7You are altogether beautiful, my
love; there is no flaw in you. 8Come with me from Lebanon, my bride; come with me from
Lebanon. Depart from the peak of Amana, from the peak of Senir and Hermon, from the
dens of lions, from the mountains of leopards. 9You have captivated my heart, my sister,
my bride; you have captivated my heart with one glance of your eyes, with one jewel of
your necklace. 10How beautiful is your love, my sister, my bride! How much better is your
love than wine, and the fragrance of your oils than any spice! 11Your lips drip nectar, my
bride; honey and milk are under your tongue; the fragrance of your garments is like the
fragrance of Lebanon. 12A garden locked is my sister, my bride, a spring locked, a fountain sealed. 13Your shoots are an orchard of pomegranates with all choicest fruits, henna
with nard, 14nard and saffron, calamus and cinnamon, with all trees of frankincense, myrrh
and aloes, with all choice spices— 15a garden fountain, a well of living water, and flowing
streams from Lebanon. 16Awake, O north wind, and come, O south wind! Blow upon my
garden, let its spices flow. Let my beloved come to his garden, and eat its choicest fruits.

DISCUSSION *Questions*

1. What is the significance of the man stopping to address her inner beauty before he mentions her outer beauty? What about the fact that he praises her beauty in a non-sexual manner before he addresses her in a more erotic manner? Which is more intimate?

"Our boy (Solomon) doesn't seem like he's in much of a hurry, does he?"

2. Summarize the world's view on sex in a few sentences or phrases.

"Insecure women who don't feel safe don't make good lovers."

3. The description of the relationship in the chapters we looked at tonight seems too good to be true. Is it? Is it feasible to have this be the love life for a married couple?

"Women aren't microwaves. They're crock pots."

4. If it is such a great scenario of what sex could be why are Christians and non-Christians alike so reluctant to strive for this?

"Sex is not only romantic, it's gentle."

5. *Married couples:* If you could give one piece of advice to engaged couples about sex , what would it be? (If preferred, you can write these on cards and give to the facilitator to read them all to the group anonymously.)

"Sex is a little scary at times, especially on this (wedding) night. Solomon is sure to put her at ease."

6. *Singles:* What can you be doing now that will make this type of sexual relationship more likely later?

"We can see from the text that Solomon is having a good time with her body. But there is something behind his desire to touch her, that is bigger than testosterone."

MEMORYVERSE

GUYS: SONG OF SOLOMON 4:7
"You are altogether beautiful, my love; there is no flaw in you."

GIRLS: SONG OF SOLOMON 4:12
"A garden locked is my sister, my bride, a spring locked, a fountain sealed."

DIVING*deeper*

Married couples: There are (at least) 4 adjectives in this chapter used to describe biblical sex: romantic, gentle, sensuous and godly. Talk with your spouse about which of these adjectives resonates the most. Can you come up with 4 other adjectives that you could use to describe ideal sex in your marriage?

Singles: Go take a cold shower. (Sorry.)

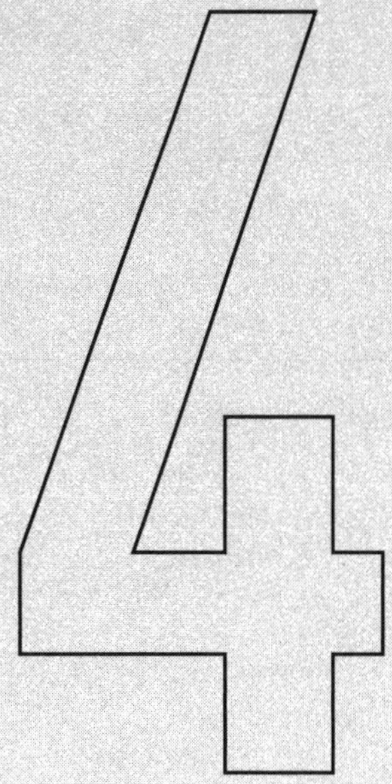

GOD *LOVES THE* *broken* ROSE

Song of Solomon 5:1

INTRO

I wanted to beat up a dad once.

I was in the deep end at a pool with my daughter, and noticed a dad and his son in the baby pool (though the kid seemed way too big to be in it). The dad was half paying attention to his kid, and half paying attention to his incoming text messages.

While my daughter and I were laughing and playing in the big pool, this poor kid could do nothing but look at us with longing eyes. He asked his dad repeatedly what that pool was. The dad kept saying, "That is not for you, buddy. You can't swim."

The boy was crushed.

"Couldn't you hold me, daddy?" The dad blew him off, told him to be quiet, and tried to convince him that the kiddie pool was the greatest thing ever. But the boy wasn't buying it for a second.

He continued to look at the big pool. He saw the kids swimming around freely, not crammed into a little tiny space. He watched as other kids got to dive out into the big, deep waters, with their daddies close by to keep them safe. He saw people jumping in and splashing in the cool, refreshing waters, and the joy in their eyes.

He got a glimpse of what swimming 'could' be, and suddenly was no longer content with his little kiddie pool.

Sex is designed to be fantastic. Once we get a glimpse of how God describes it in this one verse, I hope we can never go back and settle for anything less.

He wants us to swim in deep, deep waters, not be bored and settle for the kiddie pool.

Let's dive in.

THE WORD

SONG OF SOLOMON 5:1

[1]I came to my garden, my sister, my bride, I gathered my myrrh with my spice, I ate my honeycomb with my honey, I drank my wine with my milk. Eat, friends, drink, and be drunk with love!

DISCUSSION *Questions*

1. *Song of Solomon 5:1a* indicates that the couple having sex has been very pleasing to Him. Does that seem like an odd statement? Does it seem that most Christians think that way- that God is pleased with great, godly, biblical, marital sex?

"We see yet again that sex is not about technique,
but about finding ourselves in the rhythm of how God commanded things to be."

2. Discuss this statement from the video and determine if you agree or disagree and why: "If you see the sex had by the couple in Song of Solomon, and the sex in a porno or romantic comedy, not a person alive would opt for the sex from the porno or romantic comedy."

"This thing (the act of biblical, marital sex) pleases God."

3. What is your 'gut-level' response to the story of the broken rose? Does it evoke anger, pain, annoyance, or confusion within you? What would you have done if you had been with me at that rally with the young woman I wanted to hear about Christ? What would you have done or said to her after the rally so that she could have understood Christ accurately?

4. Put yourself in the situation of being at the young woman's hospital bed when she asked, "Is that what I am? A broken rose?" How would you respond?

"Jesus deeply and desperately loves the broken rose with no petals left."

5. "Jesus loves us no matter what – even when we are at our worst." Some take this as license to sin, while others make it purely an emotion. Still others refuse to speak this way, for fear that someone might use it as a license to sin or get very emotional about the relationship. Talk about how a communicator of this truth should handle teaching it carefully and accurately.

"I'd always been confused by church. What are we celebrating?
We are celebrating that while we are at our worst, Jesus loves us."

6. Do people tend to see the Christian faith as humans maintaining a moral code? How can believers keep from slipping into that trap?

"What we celebrate is not that 'we can' but that 'Christ did'. That is the big deal here."

"Jesus is better than everything. Than life. And there is something really freeing about that."

MEMORY VERSE

SONG OF SOLOMON 5:1

"I came to my garden, my sister, my bride, I gathered my myrrh with my spice, I ate my honeycomb with my honey, I drank my wine with my milk. Eat, friends, drink, and be drunk with love!"

DIVING *deeper*

Homework: Who in your life is someone that feels like a broken, dirty rose and needs to hear about Jesus? Who believes that they are too far gone to be saved? Pray for them. If you are really bold…approach them and tell them the Truth.

CONFLICT *will define* *YOUR* MARRIAGE

HOW ARE YOU GOING TO HANDLE IT? (PT.1)

Song of Solomon 5:2-6:3

INTRO

Suppose that you have no option but to drive down this particular dirt road in order to reach a destination. From a distance you notice that there is a large part of the road that is completely loose gravel. You are already going about 40 miles per hour, and clearly this presents a virtually unavoidable road hazard.

What should you do to prepare?

You can slow down, move over to the other side of the road, double-check your seat belt, check for a different road, tell the family to 'hold on', or barrel straight ahead and hope for the best.

The tough part of this journey is inevitable. You see it right in front of your face. The difference is that you can choose to be cautious or reckless, or somewhere in the middle.

Guess what else is inevitable in marriage: conflict. Sorry to burst your bubble, non-married people, but it is coming in all relationships, especially marriages.

It is there in front of you, but the choice is yours. How will you respond? You can plow forward, insensitively throwing caution to the wind, or you can slow down and handle the inevitable with grace.

Guess which one we are supposed to do?

THE WORD

SONG OF SOLOMON 5:2-6:3

[2]I slept, but my heart was awake. A sound! My beloved is knocking."Open to me, my sister, my love, my dove, my perfect one, for my head is wet with dew, my locks with the drops of the night." [3]I had put off my garment; how could I put it on? I had bathed my feet; how could I soil them? [4]My beloved put his hand to the latch, and my heart was thrilled within me. [5]I arose to open to my beloved, and my hands dripped with myrrh, my fingers with liquid myrrh, on the handles of the bolt. [6]I opened to my beloved, but my beloved had turned and gone. My soul failed me when he spoke. I sought him, but found him not; I called him, but he gave no answer. [7]The watchmen found me as they went about in the city; they beat me, they bruised me, they took away my veil, those watchmen of the walls. [8]I adjure you, O daughters of Jerusalem, if you find my beloved, that you tell him I am sick with love. [9]What is your beloved more than another beloved, O most beautiful among women? What is your beloved more than another beloved, that you thus adjure us? [10]My beloved is radiant and ruddy, distinguished among ten thousand. [11]His head is the finest gold; his locks are wavy, black as a raven. [12]His eyes are like doves beside streams of water, bathed in milk, sitting beside a full pool. [13]His cheeks are like beds of spices, mounds of sweet-smelling herbs. His lips are lilies, dripping liquid myrrh. [14]His arms are rods of gold, set with jewels. His body is polished ivory, bedecked with sapphires. [15]His legs are alabaster columns, set on bases of gold. His appearance is like Lebanon, choice as the cedars. [16]His mouth is most sweet, and he is altogether desirable. This is my beloved and this is my friend, O daughters of Jerusalem.

SONG OF SOLOMON 6

[1]Where has your beloved gone, O most beautiful among women? Where has your beloved turned, that we may seek him with you? [2]My beloved has gone down to his garden to the beds of spices, to graze in the gardens and to gather lilies. [3]I am my beloved's and my beloved is mine; he grazes among the lilies.

DISCUSSION *Questions*

1. We looked at the idea of not over-reacting when there are problems, frustration and fights. Is this realistic? How can this practically, tangibly play out for a married couple? A dating or engaged couple?

"The only people who think that marriage will not have a lot of conflict in it are engaged people. In that blissful state, there is a little bit of an inability to see."

2. She tells him that he is tired, and what she means is "I am tired". In other words, she is not forthright with him. What are the dangers of using 'code' (saying something but meaning another) in a relationship?

"All frustration is birthed out of unmet expectation."

3. She went from cold and unresponsive to seeking him out in the middle of the night. What could change a woman's heart to be more responsive and warm?

4. *Guys:* Loving her as Christ loved the church is our mandate, yet that is difficult as we generally want to love her to get something in return. Why is this so difficult? What is the remedy to become men that can love her simply because we are called to?

"One of the tell-tale signs of pride is that you compare your strengths to your spouses weaknesses."

5. Take some time and just process the 'nevers'. Which of these seem most dangerous? Anything to add or subtract?

Never:

- speak rashly to your mate
- touch your mate in anger
- embarrass your mate publicly
- argue in front of your kids, or use your kids to win an argument
- mention the in-laws

"Way too many men, and even more women want to use common sense arguments and manipulation to change the way their spouse feels or responds towards them. And this is going to be absolutely devastating in the end."

6. Keeping the issue on what the issue really is, is difficult isn't it? How strong is the temptation in your life to make it bigger than it really is ? ("You are as dumb as your dad.") Why do we do this and how destructive can it be?

"Only the Holy Spirit of God can change your spouse's heart. Period."

7. Do you know some couples that fight well? Remember: this would include not just how they interact in public, but also how they handle conflict in private.

MEMORY VERSE

SONG OF SOLOMON 5:8
"I adjure you, O daughters of Jerusalem, if you find my beloved, that you tell him I am sick with love."

DIVING *deeper*

HOMEWORK: For your significant other, make a list of ten things – yes, TEN things – that he/she is great at. Then let him or her know. (Dig deep, fellas…)

PRAYER *Requests*

CONFLICT *will define* *YOUR* MARRIAGE

HOW ARE YOU GOING TO HANDLE IT? (PT.2)

Song of Solomon 6:4-6:13

INTRO

If you step on a crack, you will break your mother's back.
If you make silly faces, your face will stick like that.
Don't swallow gum, unless you want it to stay in your stomach for seven years.
Breaking a mirror brings seven years of bad luck.
Storing batteries in the fridge will make them last longer.
The earth is flat.
If you eat an apple each day, the doctor will, in fact, stay away.
Marriage means the end of conflict, cause – hey – you are in love!

What do all of the above have in common? These are all lies that, at one point in history, have been widely accepted as true.

Why do we buy the fact that once we meet our best friend, the love of our life, our spouse, everything will be roses all the time? Why do we delude ourselves into thinking that once we take two sinners under the same roof and same bed – all will be well? The recipe for disaster in any relationship is to spend more time with them. As proximity increases, frustration generally increases as well.

The world tricks us into thinking that getting married means the absence of conflict. But we know better.

Right?

THE WORD

SONG OF SOLOMON 6:4-13

[4]You are beautiful as Tirzah, my love, lovely as Jerusalem, awesome as an army with banners. [5]Turn away your eyes from me, for they overwhelm me— Your hair is like a flock of goats leaping down the slopes of Gilead. [6]Your teeth are like a flock of ewes that have come up from the washing; all of them bear twins; not one among them has lost its young. [7]Your cheeks are like halves of a pomegranate behind your veil. [8]There are sixty queens and eighty concubines, and virgins without number. [9]My dove, my perfect one, is the only one, the only one of her mother, pure to her who bore her. The young women saw her and called her blessed; the queens and concubines also, and they praised her. [10]"Who is this who looks down like the dawn, beautiful as the moon, bright as the sun, awesome as an army with banners?" [11]I went down to the nut orchard to look at the blossoms of the valley, to see whether the vines had budded, whether the pomegranates were in bloom. [12]Before I was aware, my desire set me among the chariots of my kinsman, a prince. [13]Return, return, O Shulammite, return, return, that we may look upon you. Why should you look upon the Shulammite, as upon a dance before two armies?

DISCUSSION *Questions*

1. We talked in this session about not getting 'historical' during conflict. But at the same time, repeated patterns in our past need to be pointed out to us so we can grow from them and see them for the habits they are. How can you avoid being historical, but still love your spouse enough to point out flaws from their past for their betterment?

"Never get historical."

2. 'Never try to win'. Wait – seriously!? Why is that easier during courtship and dating than when you are married?

"When you get in to that mode of 'no, I am right', and there is not going to be any moving – there's not going to be any humility – and you are assured that you are right. 100% sure. That's when you get yourself in a lot of trouble."

3. It is important to note that words do hurt men, despite our best attempts to act like they do not. If we could be really honest, do you feel that words hurt men just as much as they hurt women? In the same way? Or does there still seem to be a difference and maybe – in general - harsh words are more devastating to women?

4. We learned about never using sex to win an argument, but are there other things besides sex that people use to win arguments? What other things are sometimes used as leverage in a fight?

"Men, we have times we have to own our part of the conflict - no matter how small that part is - to bring some semblance of peace to the home before we go to sleep. Lest you let the devil have a playground in your home the second you close your eyes."

5. On one hand, we are supposed to never let the sun go down on our anger *(Eph 4:26)*, but it is so hard to have productive conversations and reconcile hurts when it gets late at night. What are the dangers of dealing with something too late at night? What are the dangers of not talking about it the next morning? What are the effects on a relationship when issues are never resolved?

"With Solomon and his wife, not only has there been forgiveness that has been established as they have come back together and had a re-stirring of romance between the two of them, but now: all of that sorrow, all that shame, all that difficulty, and all that pain that both of them endured through this process has turned to dancing."

6. Time for some open discussion on the 7 steps of listening. Are there some that tend to be more difficult for men? For women? Do some seem to be more destructive than others in general? Are there any that you can think of that need to be added to the list that you observe in other marriages, (not your perfect one of course)?

1. Listen with your face
2. Don't use reason to overpower feelings
3. Don't argue
4. Don't interrupt
5. Don't leave
6. Don't go talk about your spouse to friends
7. Don't use rude body language

"Conflict is going to be one of those things that defines what happens in our marriage."

MEMORYVERSE

SONG OF SOLOMON 6:10
"Who is this who looks down like the dawn, beautiful as the moon, bright as the sun, awesome as an army with banners?"

DIVING*deeper*

Are there landmines (unresolved, un-discussed conflict and sources of pain) waiting to go off in your home? Stick it to satan and discuss them tonight. Lovingly get them out in the open so you can grow more deeply in love than ever before.

PRAYER*Requests*

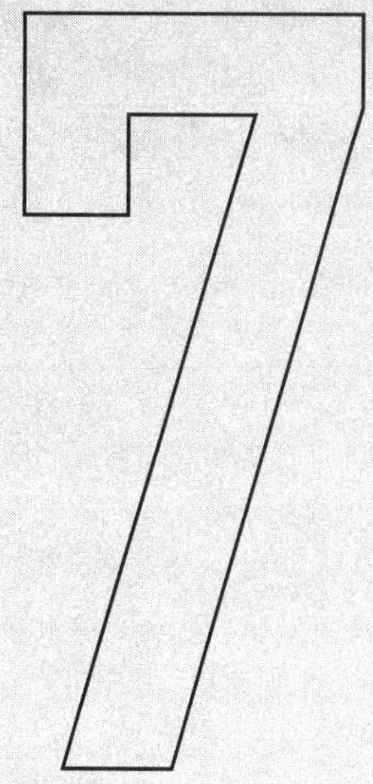

10 THINGS *to deepen* ROMANCE

Song of Solomon 7:1-8:4

INTRO

Ah...Romance.

Wait…what is 'romance' anyway? If you ask a hundred people what romance is, you will probably get a hundred different responses. What is romance?

One dictionary defines a 'romance' (as in, a romantic story) as: "something (as an extravagant story or account) that lacks basis in fact"[1] (Emphasis mine.)

Romance, something that permeates so much of our culture today, has its etymology in a particular type of story: a heroic, adventurous, mysterious, story, that is so outlandish, that it lacks any basis in fact. These are the types of stories that every little girl grows up reading and picturing herself in. She is the princess, and there will someday be a prince to sweep her off her feet.

These little girls become grown up girls who like romance. Guys like girls, so we act like we like it.

You don't need to conduct any research to know that guys, in general, don't really 'do' romance instinctively.

Girls love it, guys stink at it. So what can we do about this?

I am glad you asked.

---

[1] Inc Merriam-Webster, Merriam-Webster's Collegiate Dictionary., Eleventh ed. (Springfield, Mass.: Merriam-Webster, Inc., 2003).

THE WORD

SONG OF SOLOMON 7:1-8:4

[1]How beautiful are your feet in sandals, O noble daughter! Your rounded thighs are like
jewels, the work of a master hand. [2]Your navel is a rounded bowl that never lacks mixed
wine. Your belly is a heap of wheat, encircled with lilies. [3]Your two breasts are like two
fawns, twins of a gazelle. [4]Your neck is like an ivory tower. Your eyes are pools in Heshbon,
by the gate of Bath-rabbim. Your nose is like a tower of Lebanon, which looks toward
Damascus. [5]Your head crowns you like Carmel, and your flowing locks are like purple; a
king is held captive in the tresses. [6]How beautiful and pleasant you are, O loved one, with
all your delights! [7]Your stature is like a palm tree, and your breasts are like its clusters. [8]I
say I will climb the palm tree and lay hold of its fruit. Oh may your breasts be like clusters
of the vine, and the scent of your breath like apples, [9]and your mouth like the best wine.
It goes down smoothly for my beloved, gliding over lips and teeth. [10]I am my beloved's,
and his desire is for me. [11]Come, my beloved, let us go out into the fields and lodge in
the villages; [12]let us go out early to the vineyards and see whether the vines have budded,
whether the grape blossoms have opened and the pomegranates are in bloom. There I
will give you my love. [13]The mandrakes give forth fragrance, and beside our doors are all
choice fruits, new as well as old, which I have laid up for you, O my beloved.

SONG OF SOLOMON 8

[1]Oh that you were like a brother to me who nursed at my mother's breasts! If I found you
outside, I would kiss you, and none would despise me. [2]I would lead you and bring you
into the house of my mother— she who used to teach me. I would give you spiced wine
to drink, the juice of my pomegranate. [3]His left hand is under my head, and his right hand
embraces me! [4]I adjure you, O daughters of Jerusalem, that you not stir up or awaken
love until it pleases.

DISCUSSION*Questions*

1. What are the benefits of acting out *Song of Solomon 6:11*, where you go out, away on a vacation, to a place without kids, dog, etc. What specifically does that do for a couple? How frequently and what type of trips could these be? Does it do the same for the man as the woman?

"Romance is a discipline. For some of us, romance springs out of this well of creativity. We usually hate those guys."

2. If the burden for romance falls to the male, and males generally do not 'romance' well, what is the solution? Should women just resolve to live their lives disappointed? Should men live completely counter to how they naturally are?

"You don't *fall* into romance. You don't *accidentally* get romantic. It's planned."

3. What is the effect of Hollywood on women's expectations of men in romance?

4. What are some examples of things you can learn about your spouse as you seek to become an 'expert' on him or her?

"The problem with church literature is that it makes everybody the same. Is that anybody's reality?"

5. How can you develop a deep appreciation for your spouse? Why specifically is this so important in a relationship?

"It's one thing to tell your spouse something that everyone knows about them. Its another to know them in such a way that you can praise them in such a way that no one else knows about."

6. What are the keys to fostering a mindset of deep respect for each other?

"Men rarely seek out non-sexual touching. If we initiate sweet touching, we are usually thinking, 'I hope this is going somewhere...'."

7. Take some time to review the ten things that can deepen romance, and let's have some open discussion: Which of these are easy? Which are more difficult? Which can be implemented quickly and readily in your relationship? Are there any that are more important in the dating years? The early days of marriage? The later years of marriage?

1. Become experts on your spouse
2. Get good at exalting your spouse
3. Praising something about him/her that only he/she knows
4. Have a deep appreciation for your spouse
5. Have a pervasive gentleness
6. Delight in your spouse
7. Have a strong devotion to one another
8. Have an immense desire for one another
9. Have some 'old ways' and some 'new ways'
10. Become an expert on your spouse's strongpoints

"The message we get from the world is that we are missing out, and that we need to experience what it is like to be with more than one lover."

"If you can know the names of all the guys on the rosters of your favorite teams, you can find a few creative ideas to try on your wife."

MEMORYVERSE

SONG OF SOLOMON 7:10
"I am my beloved's, and his desire is for me."

DIVING*deeper*

HOMEWORK FOR MEN: Make a list of 5 things that you can do to be romantic and creative with your girl. (Ask around. Google. You can do it.) Make a plan over the next month or so to do all five things – with no expectations from her in return.

HOMEWORK FOR WOMEN: Think of an area where you might have unrealistic expectations of your man. Grab coffee with a girlfriend and talk about expectations in general, but specifically process with her this area where you have too high of expectations for him.

PRAYER*Requests*

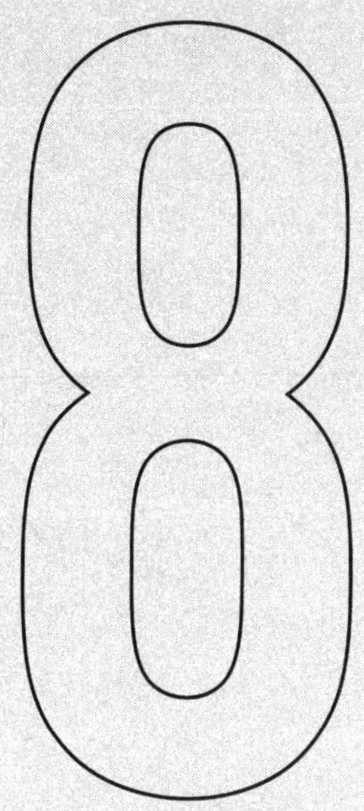

I LOVE *you* & I AM NOT GOING ANYWHERE

Song of Solomon 8:5-14

INTRO

OPTION 1:

My marriage is boring. I'm out.
This is not the life I signed on for with my spouse. I'm out.
He is not near as sweet to me as I thought he would be. I'm out.
She is not as sexy as I thought she would be. I'm out.
This is harder than I thought. I'm out.
I have no freedom. I'm out.
I hate being around the house. I'm out.
You should hear the way my spouse talks to me. I'm out.
This is miserable. I'm out.
It would be so much easier to just start over instead of fixing all our issues. I'm out.
This relationship absolutely, unequivocally, stinks. I'm out.

OPTION 2:

Right now, my marriage might be the most difficult, boring, draining, crippling thing ever...but I'm all in.

And I'm not
going
anywhere.

THE WORD

SONG OF SOLOMON 8:5-14

5Who is that coming up from the wilderness, leaning on her beloved? Under the apple
tree I awakened you. There your mother was in labor with you; there she who bore you
was in labor. 6Set me as a seal upon your heart, as a seal upon your arm, for love is strong
as death, jealousy is fierce as the grave. Its flashes are flashes of fire, the very flame of the
LORD. 7Many waters cannot quench love, neither can floods drown it. If a man offered
for love all the wealth of his house, he would be utterly despised. 8We have a little sister,
and she has no breasts. What shall we do for our sister on the day when she is spoken
for? 9If she is a wall, we will build on her a battlement of silver, but if she is a door, we will
enclose her with boards of cedar. 10I was a wall, and my breasts were like towers; then I
was in his eyes as one who finds peace. 11Solomon had a vineyard at Baal-hamon; he let
out the vineyard to keepers; each one was to bring for its fruit a thousand pieces of silver.
12My vineyard, my very own, is before me; you, O Solomon, may have the thousand, and
the keepers of the fruit two hundred. 13O you who dwell in the gardens, with companions
listening for your voice; let me hear it. 14Make haste, my beloved, and be like a gazelle or
a young stag on the mountains of spices.

DISCUSSION *Questions*

1. Solomon was far from perfect. In fact we alluded to Ecclesiastes in which Solomon tries money, parties, gardening, building huge homes and more to find satisfaction. What are other things that people use to find satisfaction? What seems to be the reason that we constantly pursue things that we know will never truly fulfill us?

"There is fantasy that you only have to imagine when you have 1,000 women at your beckon call. You get anything you want...Although it sounds like a dream to our culture, Solomon found it to be exhausting, painful, gut-wrenching, and full of regret."

2. What patterns or expectations have you brought into your relationships that are unconsciously from your family? (Some categories might be: expectations about money, church, roles of the husband or a wife, philosophies about children, and more.)

"Things can't get darker. *I'm not going anywhere.*
You couldn't hurt me any more. *I'm not going anywhere.*
You couldn't betray me any farther. *I'm not going anywhere.*"

3. You hear some transparency in my saying, 'at work I am a big deal'. Contrast that to some years in my marriage where I did not want to come home, because of my frustrations with my wife. What would you have told young Chandler in those days if you could have given me counsel?

"There is something about a ferocity of commitment that gets us to the place where love and intimacy can be at its deepest when you are not allowed to go anywhere."

4. What moved me for the first time to call a Christian counselor was Lauren's (my wife's) kindness towards me. It was not a nagging but a hug and tender words. Why is it that we know that is effective, but we resort to arguing and proving our case to our loved ones in order to move them to action? Why do we resort to nagging or overpowering our spouse when we know that tenderness will work?

"At the end of the day, this thing is about Jesus. At the end of the day, this thing has to be about Jesus because He is our only hope for reconciliation."

5. Take some time and sum up the teaching of this session in a few sentences and share it with the group.

6. What has been the greatest benefit of this study for you as an individual or a couple? Are there any new patterns that have emerged in your relationship as a result?

"Religion, if it had a bumper sticker, would say, "I do, therefore I am accepted'. That's not Christianity. Christianity is "God did. Christ did. So I am accepted.' It's completely opposite."

MEMORYVERSE

SONG OF SOLOMON 8:6
"Set me as a seal upon your heart, as a seal upon your arm, for love is strong as death, jealousy is fierce as the grave. Its flashes are flashes of fire, the very flame of the LORD."

DIVING*deeper*

HOMEWORK FOR MARRIED COUPLES: Dig up your wedding vows and read them to each other. Remember what you promised to each other, and pray together that God helps you keep that commitment for a lifetime.

HOMEWORK FOR DATING, ENGAGED & SINGLES: Find a person that has been married for a long time (25+ years). Take them to lunch, dinner, etc. and ask them questions about what it is like to be married for that long. What are the most vital things to do to thrive in your marriage? What are the biggest mistakes you could make someday if you get married?

PRAYER *Requests*

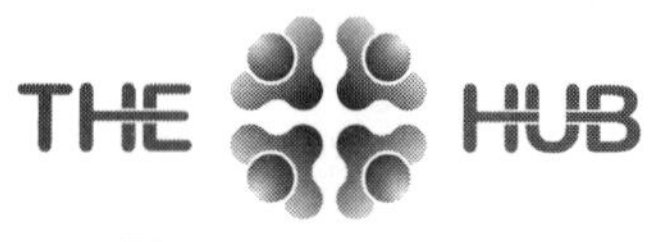

NEW! Philippians

To Live is Christ & to Die is Gain

Video Teaching Series. Buy. Rent. Download.

The story begins in Philippi. Where Paul introduces three individuals that were all enslaved by the kind of things we often choose over the gospel.

- Lydia, the Business Executive
- The Little Slave Girl
- The Hard Working Jailer

Their lives portray dysfunction and emptiness but are totally transformed by the Gospel. True joy and Christ's love begin to live within them, giving them a life of purpose.

In fact, Paul himself was enslaved and then by God's grace and mercy he could pen these popular and profound words:

To live is Christ & to die is gain
I can do all things through Christ who strengthens me

Let's join Matt Chandler, Pastor of The Village Church in Dallas, Texas, as he walks us through Philippians. In this, one of the most intimate of Paul's letters, he paints a beautiful picture of what it is to be a mature Christian.

About

MATT CHANDLER serves as Lead Pastor of The Village Church in Highland Village, TX. He describes his tenure at The Village as a re-planting effort where he was involved in changing the theological and philosophical culture of the congregation. The church has witnessed a tremendous response growing from 160 people to over 8,000 including satellite campuses in Dallas and Denton. He is one of the most downloaded teachers on iTunes and consistently remains in the Top 5 of all national Religion and Spirituality Podcasts. Matt's passion is to speak to people in America and abroad about the glory of God and beauty of Jesus.

His greatest joy outside of Jesus is being married to Lauren and being a dad to their three children, Audrey, Reid and Norah.

NEW! Love Life

Song of Solomon

Video Teaching Series. Buy. Rent. Download.

What does it really mean to love? What does love look like in singleness, dating or marriage?

Through the study of Song of Solomon, Mark Driscoll reveals an Old Testament understanding of biblical sexuality with current cultural clarity.

Learn to celebrate God's gift of love in all of life by walking through this timely series.

About

PASTOR MARK DRISCOLL founded Mars Hill Church in Seattle in the fall of 1996. The church has grown from a small Bible study to over 10,000 people. He co-founded and is president of the Acts 29 Church Planting Network which has planted over 200 churches. He has authored The Radical Reformission, Death by Love, Religion Saves, Doctrine and many more.

Most of all, Mark and his high school sweetheart, Grace, enjoy raising their three sons and two daughters.

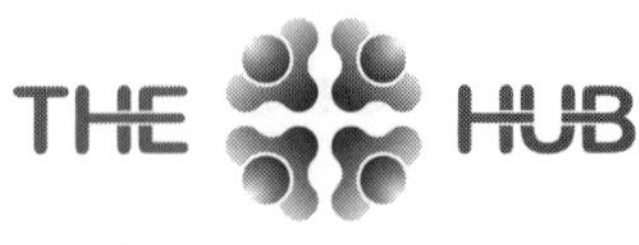

Song of Solomon 2005

Video Teaching Series. Buy. Rent. Download.

Used and loved throughout the world, the Song of Solomon series teaches the biblical design for relationships. For both singles and married couples, this study follows Solomon's relationship from attraction to dating and courtship, marriage and intimacy to resolving conflict, keeping romance alive and committing to the end. The 10th Anniversary Edition (released in 2005) updates Tommy Nelson's original study with updated teaching and added features.

SOS for Students

Video Teaching Series. Buy. Rent. Download.

Every parent, student pastor and student know the absolute need of saying, "an ounce of prevention is worth a pound of cure." God gave us the gift of love, marriage and sexuality, but since Christians have been mostly silent on this issue, many students learn these things from the secular community. As a result, students have a distorted view of sexuality and God's purpose for it.

Song of Solomon for Students teaches that God is for love and sexuality; in fact, it is His design and gift in the first place. Tommy Nelson taught these 6, 25 minute sessions to junior and senior high students. It will walk them through the first four chapters of Song of Solomon and focuses on these issues: attraction, dating and the truth about sexuality and when it is most enjoyed and most honoring to God.

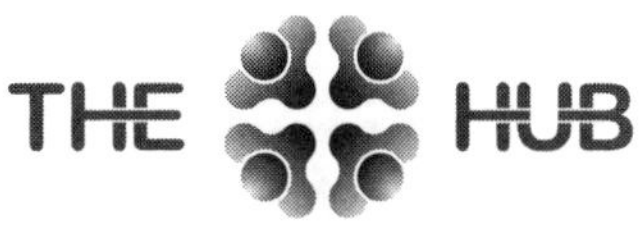

Romans, Volume I & II

The Letter that Changed the World

Video Teaching Series. Buy. Rent. Download.

The most important idea in the Bible is how a Holy God can get a sinful man into Heaven and not compromise who He is. Romans tell us just that! It sits as Master of the House before all of Paul's writings. It is the Bible in miniature. It is the most important singular document ever penned by man and only inspiration could make it so.

In our study in Romans we will look at Paul's unfolding logic and incisive reasoning as to the divinity and holiness of the Christian gospel. When this book has been understood, reformation and new life follow shortly.

About

TOMMY NELSON has been the Pastor of Denton Bible Church, in Denton, Texas, since 1977. Tommy graduated from the University of North Texas with a Bachelor's Degree in Education. He then attended Dallas Theological Seminary in Dallas, Texas, where he received the Master of Arts in Biblical Studies degree.

Tommy has been married to Teresa since 1974. They have two grown sons, Ben and John, along with five grandchildren.

NEW! Ruth

A True Story of Love & Redemption

Video Teaching Series. Buy. Rent. Download.

Ruth is a courageous woman. Boaz is a generous man. Both exemplified great character. Ruth needed a redeemer. We all need a redeemer.

The Book of Ruth is simply put the greatest love story, ever. Tommy Nelson, Author, Pastor, and Teacher will lead us through this compelling story of Romance & Redemption.

In this journey you will learn:

- The Character of a Great Woman
- The Character of a Great Man
- How to Find God's Will for Life
- Your Redeemer
- Our King

About

TOMMY NELSON has been the pastor of Denton Bible Church, in Denton, Texas, since 1977. Tommy graduated from the University of North Texas with a Bachelor's Degree in Education. He then attended Dallas Theological Seminary in Dallas, Texas, where he received the Master of Arts in Biblical Studies degree.

Tommy has been married to Teresa Nelson since 1974. They have two grown sons, Ben and John, along with five grandchildren.

Vintage Jesus

Timeless Answers to Timely Questions

Video Teaching Series. Buy. Rent. Download.

Who do you say I am?

There is no greater question. No one is more loved and hated than Jesus. "To some an aroma of life, to others an aroma of death."

The Vintage Jesus Study Guide will drive you to the scriptures in search of Who Jesus Really Is by answering 12 of the most pressing questions about the nature, humanity and deity of our Saviour.

Author and Pastor Mark Driscoll uses humor, expertise, boldness and relevance with today's culture to help lead us to answer this question correctly.

Perhaps unlike any other Teaching Curriculum, Vintage Jesus will equip Christians to have more understanding and confidence in communicating the deity and life changing power of Jesus. For those who are seeking the Ultimate Truth of life, with relevance and grace, this series will cause everyone to think hard about Jesus' own question that He asked thousands of years ago, "Who Do You Say That I AM?"

About

PASTOR MARK DRISCOLL founded Mars Hill Church in Seattle in the fall of 1996. The church has grown from a small Bible study to over 10,000 people. He co-founded and is president of the Acts 29 Church Planting Network which has planted over 200 churches. He has authored The Radical Reformission, Death by Love, Religion Saves, Doctrine and many more.

Most of all, Mark and his high school sweetheart, Grace, enjoy raising their three sons and two daughters.

NOTES